*Greater Than a Tourist Books are also available in Ebook and Audiobook format.

Greater Than a Tourist Book Series
Reviews from Readers

I think the series is wonderful and beneficial for tourists to get information before visiting the city.

-Seckin Zumbul, Izmir Turkey

I am a world traveler who has read many trip guides but this one really made a difference for me. I would call it a heartfelt creation of a local guide expert instead of just a guide.

-Susy, Isla Holbox, Mexico

New to the area like me, this is a must have!

 -Joe, Bloomington, USA

This is a good series that gets down to it when looking for things to do at your destination without having to read a novel for just a few ideas.

-Rachel, Monterey, USA

Good information to have to plan my trip to this destination.

-Pennie Farrell, Mexico

Great ideas for a port day.
-Mary Martin USA

Aptly titled, you won't just be a tourist after reading this book. You'll be greater than a tourist!
-Alan Warner, Grand Rapids, USA

Even though I only have three days to spend in San Miguel in an upcoming visit, I will use the author's suggestions to guide some of my time there. An easy read - with chapters named to guide me in directions I want to go.
 -Robert Catapano, USA

Great insights from a local perspective! Useful information and a very good value!
 -Sarah, USA

This series provides an in-depth experience through the eyes of a local. Reading these series will help you to travel the city in with confidence and it'll make your journey a unique one.
-Andrew Teoh, Ipoh, Malaysia

\>TOURIST

GREATER THAN A TOURIST- CHARLOTTE NORTH CAROLINA USA

50 Travel Tips from a Local

Erik Drew

Greater Than a Tourist- Charlotte, NC USA Copyright © 2019 by CZYK Publishing LLC. All Rights Reserved.

All rights reserved. No part of this book may be reproduced in any form or by any electronic or mechanical means including information storage and retrieval systems, without permission in writing from the author. The only exception is by a reviewer, who may quote short excerpts in a review.

The statements in this book are of the authors and may not be the views of CZYK Publishing or Greater Than a Tourist.

Cover designed by: Ivana Stamenkovic
Cover Image: https://pixabay.com/photos/charlotte-north-carolina-city-3994040/

CZYK Publishing Since 2011.

Greater Than a Tourist

Lock Haven, PA
All rights reserved.

ISBN: 9781712468838

>TOURIST

50 TRAVEL TIPS FROM A LOCAL

\>TOURIST

BOOK DESCRIPTION

Are you excited about planning your next trip? Do you want to try something new? Would you like some guidance from a local? If you answered yes to any of these questions, then this Greater Than a Tourist book is for you. *Greater Than a Tourist-Charlotte, North Carolina USA* by Author Erik Drew offers the inside scoop on Charlotte. Most travel books tell you how to travel like a tourist. Although there is nothing wrong with that, as part of the Greater Than a Tourist series, this book will give you travel tips from someone who has lived at your next travel destination.

In these pages, you will discover advice that will help you throughout your stay. This book will not tell you exact addresses or store hours but instead will give you excitement and knowledge from a local that you may not find in other smaller print travel books.

Travel like a local. Slow down, stay in one place, and get to know the people and culture. By the time you finish this book, you will be eager and prepared to travel to your next destination.

Inside this travel guide book you will find:

- Insider tips from a local.
- Packing and planning list.
- List of travel questions to ask yourself or others while traveling.
- A place to write your travel bucket list.

OUR STORY

Traveling is a passion of the Greater than a Tourist book series creator. Lisa studied abroad in college, and for their honeymoon Lisa and her husband toured Europe. During her travels to Malta, an older man tried to give her some advice based on his own experience living on the island since he was a young boy. She was not sure if she should talk to the stranger but was interested in his advice. When traveling to some places she was wary to talk to locals because she was afraid that they weren't being genuine. Through her travels, Lisa learned how much locals had to share with tourists. Lisa created the Greater Than a Tourist book series to help connect people with locals. A topic that locals are very passionate about sharing.

>TOURIST

TABLE OF CONTENTS

BOOK DESCRIPTION

OUR STORY

TABLE OF CONTENTS

DEDICATION

ABOUT THE AUTHOR

HOW TO USE THIS BOOK

FROM THE PUBLISHER

WELCOME TO

> TOURIST

INTRODUCTION

1. Carowinds Is Fun For Everyone, But Eat Before You Go
2. Scarowinds Is Fun For September And October Visits, But Go On A Friday Night
3. WinterFest Should Be On Your December Itinerary
4. Charlotte Has An Amazing Brewery Culture
5. Sycamore Brewing Has The Best Outdoor Area
6. Suffolk Punch Is The Brewery With The Best Food
7. White Zombie Is (Arguably) The Best Local Beer
8. Self-Serve Lounges Are The New Trend, But They Are Always More Expensive
9. Hoppin' Is Fun For Wednesday Night Bingo

10. South End Is Home To A Young, Vibrant Area Of Charlotte
11. Leroy Fox Is A Popular Restaurant In South End
12. Jeni's Ice Cream Is Perfect For Your Instagram
13. LGBTQ Nightlife
14. NoDa Is Perfect For The Artsy Types
15. Pop Bar
16. Take A Breather Or Some Pictures In The Beautiful Romare Bearden Park
17. Charlotte Knights Are An Inexpensive, Fun Experience
18. Enjoy The Post-Game Fireworks At Friday And Saturday Knights' Games
19. The Knights Have Thursday And Sunday Promotions Too
20. If You Plan Ahead The Carolina Panthers Games Are Always Fun
21. Graham Street Pub And Patio Is A Really Cool Spot For a Pregame Drink
22. Latta Arcade / The French Quarter Is Unique And Fun
23. Zablong Is Open Late And Delicious
24. Charlotte Has Some Awesome Irish Bars
25. Charlotte's EpiCentre Is A Fun Spot
26. The EpiCentre Is Not Family Friendly After 9pm Thursday - Saturday

>TOURIST

27. Rooftop 210 Rarely Has A Cover
28. Fuji Has The Best Takeout Hibachi
29. Johnny Burrito Is A Legendary Charlotte Lunch Spot
30. Omni Hotel Coin Bar Has A Public Rooftop Pool
31. Merchant And Trade Is An Upscale Rooftop Bar Perfect For Drinks
32. City Lights Is Another Great Rooftop Cocktail Bar
33. Take It Back To The 90's At Roxbury Nightclub
34. Dandelion Market Is One Of The Most Popular Places In Charlotte
35. Charlotte Hornets Games Are Fun And Not Crazy Expensive
36. Attending A Hornets Game? Fitzgerald's Is Also A Great Pregame Spot For Food And Drinks
37. UNC Charlotte Has A Scenic Campus You Should Visit
38. UNC Charlotte Football Games Are Fun And Cheap
39. Workman's Friend Has Phenomenal Grilled Cheese And Tomato Soup
40. Rosemont Has Adult Caprisun Style Drinks
41. South Park Mall Is A Premiere Shopping Destination

42. Quail Hollow Should Be On The Bucket List For Any Golfer
43. Ballantyne Corporate Park Has Plenty Of Scenic Walking Trails
44. Alexander Michael's "What It Is" Dish Must Be Tried
45. Benny Pennello's Pizza Is Massive… Literally
46. South End's Charlotte Rail Trail Is A Hotspot
47. The U.S. National Whitewater Center Is A Fun Destination For The Day
48. Taco Tuesday At Hot Taco
49. The Charlotte Checkers Games Are Affordable And Exciting
50. The Billy Graham Library Is A Popular Tourist Destination
51. Charlotte's New Optimist Hall Is A Foodie's Dream

TOP REASONS TO BOOK THIS TRIP

Other Resources:

Packing and Planning Tips

Travel Questions

Travel Bucket List

NOTES

>TOURIST

DEDICATION

This book is dedicated to Andrew Gallimore, who I've shared so many fun and crazy experiences with here in Charlotte.

ABOUT THE AUTHOR

Erik Drew is a local Charlotte resident who lives right in the heart of the city. He loves to be social and experience the many local breweries, restaurants, and events that Charlotte has to offer. You can always find him out and about in Uptown or South End, especially on weekends. Born in Massachusetts, his family moved to Charlotte while he was attending college at Ole Miss in Oxford, Mississippi. After graduation, he moved to Charlotte and has loved everything about living in the Queen City.

>TOURIST

HOW TO USE THIS BOOK

The *Greater Than a Tourist* book series was written by someone who has lived in an area for over three months. The goal of this book is to help travelers either dream or experience different locations by providing opinions from a local. The author has made suggestions based on their own experiences. Please check before traveling to the area in case the suggested places are unavailable.

Travel Advisories: As a first step in planning any trip abroad, check the Travel Advisories for your intended destination.
https://travel.state.gov/content/travel/en/traveladvisories/traveladvisories.html

FROM THE PUBLISHER

Traveling can be one of the most important parts of a person's life. The anticipation and memories that you have are some of the best. As a publisher of the Greater Than a Tourist, as well as the popular *50 Things to Know* book series, we strive to help you learn about new places, spark your imagination, and inspire you. Wherever you are and whatever you do I wish you safe, fun, and inspiring travel.

Lisa Rusczyk Ed. D.
CZYK Publishing

>TOURIST

```
WELCOME TO
> TOURIST
```

>TOURIST

INTRODUCTION

"I'm in love with cities I've never been to and people I've never met."

-John Green

Charlotte, North Carolina is a beautiful modern city that is quickly growing as more and more people and companies realize how amazing it is. There is a young, trendy vibe in Charlotte with plenty of fun places to visit. The Queen City is the perfect medium-sized metropolitan, with a gorgeous skyline and NFL stadium that gives you the big city feel while still remaining easy to navigate. New places to eat, drink, and shop are always opening up - making this such a fun city to explore. There are plenty of fun activities and places to check out, here are my personal tips to help you on your next Charlotte trip!

Charlotte
North Carolina, USA

Charlotte Climate

	High	Low
January	51	31
February	56	34
March	64	41
April	73	49
May	80	57
June	86	66
July	90	69
August	88	68
September	82	62
October	72	50
November	63	40
December	54	34

GreaterThanaTourist.com

Temperatures are in Fahrenheit degrees.
Source: NOAA

1. CAROWINDS IS FUN FOR EVERYONE, BUT EAT BEFORE YOU GO

Carowinds, the amusement park located on the border of North Carolina and South Carolina, has one of the coolest roller coasters in Fury 325. This amusement park has entertainment for all ages, and I definitely recommend conquering Fury 325 at least once while you visit Charlotte. The coaster gets its name from the 325 foot drop at the start of the ride. If you aren't too scared, take a look while you are climbing up the lift hill, the view is amazing and you can see Uptown in the distance! Intimidator is another fun coaster if you are looking for even more thrills! Check out the free shows in the theater throughout the day. Make sure you eat before you go, as the dining options are a bit pricey for those without a year-long meal plan. There are plenty of food options nearby, including a rare Moe's Southwestern Grill with a drive-thru!

>TOURIST

2. SCAROWINDS IS FUN FOR SEPTEMBER AND OCTOBER VISITS, BUT GO ON A FRIDAY NIGHT

Carowinds goes through a major transformation every September and October into a Halloween metropolis called Scarowinds. Haunted houses, spooky shows, and nighttime rides on the roller coasters all make Scarowinds worthwhile, but make sure you visit on a Friday night. The event is only open from 7pm - midnight on the weekends, but Saturday night tends to be MUCH busier than Friday nights. Scarowinds is my favorite time of year for Carowinds, and it's honestly a ton of fun. The haunted houses are professional enough to be scary without being too intense. The lines for the haunted houses can be a bit long, so plan out which ones you want to hit ahead of time so you don't miss out. Carowinds spares nothing with their decorations, and the entertainment and shows are awesome!

3. WINTERFEST SHOULD BE ON YOUR DECEMBER ITINERARY

Visiting in December? Carowinds has a phenomenal holiday spectacular complete with Christmas lights, the Polar Express parade, and ice skating. You can decorate cookies with Mrs. Claus while drinking hot cocoa. Some of the rides are also open during the annual holiday event, it's a must-visit for any December visit. The only true roller coaster open during WinterFest is After Burn, so don't expect to ride Fury 325 or Intimidator. The horse-drawn carriage ride does have an additional fee, along with the ice skating. The Christmas lights are breathtaking and the shows are incredible. This is truly fun for the entire family!

>TOURIST

4. CHARLOTTE HAS AN AMAZING BREWERY CULTURE

Charlotte has close to 50 local breweries! You'll find a lot of people at these breweries on Friday and Saturday afternoons, as most have large taprooms they serve their beer at. These are also some of the best places to see the cutest dogs, as customers often bring their furry friends with them! Local breweries are where Charlotte residents go to socialize, play games, and support the local economy. Brewery culture is so strong in Charlotte that more and more open up each year, which is truly awesome having so many local options here. Most local Charlotte breweries even have a running club or yoga class they offer where anyone is welcome to join. These clubs always enjoy a friendly beer after their group exercise, what could be better?

5. SYCAMORE BREWING HAS THE BEST OUTDOOR AREA

Sycamore Brewing in South End has the most popular outdoor area. Located right on the Rail Trail, people often walk or take an electric scooter here to enjoy some awesome beer. Friday's (excluding the winter) are Food Truck Fridays, where food trucks line up in this outdoor area with some amazing food. Sunday afternoons are referred to as "Front Porch Sundays," and have local vendors selling handmade goods. It's really neat to explore the different vendors while enjoying Sycamore's delicious beer! One of the usual vendors at Front Porch Sundays is Glory Days Apparel, which has some really cool Charlotte themed shirts and sweatshirts. My favorite year-long beer at Sycamore is Sun Grown, an easy-drinking light beer that has won numerous awards. Their Pumpkin Latte Blonde beer that's available during the autumn months is phenomenal. The Lil' IPA is a unique blend of a Pilsner and IPA that has under 100 calories but is honestly full of flavor. Recently Sycamore came out with their own brands of coffee (Beach Shack Coffee) and spiked seltzer (Bubs) that are both worth a try at their South End brewery location. Their Wild Blossom Cider brand is also on tap at their brewery location and very popular. Sycamore is hands down my favorite brewery in Charlotte, from the beer selection and variation to the atmosphere itself... you must visit while you're here!

6. SUFFOLK PUNCH IS THE BREWERY WITH THE BEST FOOD

Suffolk Punch is just down the Rail Trail (a scenic walking path through South End) from Sycamore. This brewery has great local beer, but they also have a phenomenal full-service food menu. This is one of the many popular brunch spots in Charlotte! Try their axe throwing lanes if you're feeling adventurous. Noble Toast, Blue Daisy, and Shovel Flag are all worth trying at Suffolk Punch. I recommend ordering a flight and trying them all! The pecan French toast dish on the weekend brunch menu is simply to die for! Pair it with a mimosa for the perfect brunch experience.

7. WHITE ZOMBIE IS (ARGUABLY) THE BEST LOCAL BEER

White Zombie, made by Catawba Brewing in the Plaza Midwood section of Charlotte, is one of the most popular local beers. If you like craft beer, you MUST try White Zombie while you're here visiting! Catawba Brewing has a large indoor taproom, perfect for those cooler temperatures. They have plenty of awesome beers to choose from, but White Zombie is by far the best. Although it sounds like a Halloween beer, it is available year-round. White Zombie is an easy-drinking white ale beer but still packs a flavorful punch.

8. SELF-SERVE LOUNGES ARE THE NEW TREND, BUT THEY ARE ALWAYS MORE EXPENSIVE

Self-serve places, like Hoppin' in South End, have a ton of taps on the wall and let you pour your own beer. How much you pour is tracked through a wristband system linked to your credit card, and you

>TOURIST

pay by the ounce. (Think self-serve frozen yogurt but for beer, wine, and cider). This sounds awesome, but it almost always ends up being more expensive than if you just ordered the same beer at regular. I find myself being charged over $7 for a normal sized craft beer, when the same beer is typically $6 at most other places. Not to mention you get charged even for taste testing a beer before you pour a full glass, something most bartenders let you do for free. The main self-serve bars in Charlotte are Hoppin' in South End and Tap Room Social in Uptown. Hoppin' tends to get a bigger crowd than Tap Room Social, but this is likely due to a more easily accessible location.

9. HOPPIN' IS FUN FOR WEDNESDAY NIGHT BINGO

Hoppin' in South End may be somewhat pricey with their self-pour prices, but they do have a fun Bingo every Wednesday night. It's free to play and you can win some sweet prizes! As a hint, it's typically music trivia where they play a song and you have to mark it on your Bingo board if you have it (and know the name of it). If you really want to win, have the Shazam app open on your phone under the table, but you didn't hear that from me. Prices range from free gear, gift cards, and even concert tickets. This is a lot of fun with a group of friends, certainly a fun activity for any Wednesday night!

10. SOUTH END IS HOME TO A YOUNG, VIBRANT AREA OF CHARLOTTE

South End has been completely revitalized, and is now the most popular section of Charlotte. The Charlotte Rail Trail runs through the heart of it, and it's home to numerous breweries, bars, and restaurants. Street art and murals adds to the beauty of this growing area just outside of Uptown. There are also plenty of shopping attractions in South End, it's a MUST visit for any Charlotte visitor! South End is booming with millenials, and the bars and restaurants seem to cater towards a younger crowd. South End is my favorite part of Charlotte, and most of my favorite breweries and restaurants are all located here. The Charlotte Rail Trail makes everything very accessible, and you'll see people riding the rideshare electric scooters or walking from place to place. You can easily use the light rail to access South End as well, with multiple Blue Line stops in the area. There is just about every type of bar in South End, whether it's a British soccer bar, an Irish bar, or a sports bar they are all there. This area thrives every weekend and it's an exciting place to experience with all it has to offer!

11. LEROY FOX IS A POPULAR RESTAURANT IN SOUTH END

Leroy Fox is a trendy restaurant with a mix of modern American food and some Southern home cooking dishes. It has a second location in Dillworth, but its South End spot is the most popular right in the heart of this vibrant area. I love their blackened grilled chicken dish, and this is one of Charlotte's most popular brunch spots as well! Try the macaroni and cheese as one of your sides, you won't regret it! This is seriously my favorite restaurant in Charlotte, the food is delicious! The food and drink prices are all extremely reasonable and won't break your budget. If you take any single recommendation from this book, make sure you visit Leroy Fox for one of your meals!

12. JENI'S ICE CREAM IS PERFECT FOR YOUR INSTAGRAM

There are three different Jeni's Ice Cream locations in Charlotte, but the South End one has the cutest aesthetic. It's so worth the long line it gets during the warmer temperatures, and perfect for an Instagram picture. The "Confetti Hearts" mural on the side of the building is a popular background for pictures. This Jeni's Ice Cream location is open year-round. Try the Frose flavor, it's amazing! Make sure you sample a few flavors before ordering, the always friendly staff will gladly help you out. Try out Hawkers Asian Street Fare which is located directly next to Jeni's South End location. This trendy Asian restaurant is usually busy so make sure you call ahead. Whether you eat your ice cream before or after dinner is up to you… I have experience with both!

>TOURIST

13. LGBTQ NIGHTLIFE

Charlotte has a handful of popular LGBTQ nightlife attractions. The Bar At 316 (a Victorian house transformed into a gay bar) in South End is busiest on Friday nights, while Bar Argon (a video dance bar with really cool decorations) is the place to go on Saturday nights. It's an odd but definitive trend, and every weekend follows that pattern. The Bar At 316 can get very crowded upstairs, especially on the stage. Just be prepared to squeeze and slide your way around if it's a popular night. They also can go a bit overboard on the fog machine, so keep that in mind if you are sensitive to it. It's essentially one big house party, and a lot of fun if you are looking to have a good time. Bar Argon is super fun with their many themed nights on Saturdays. I swear this place must spend a ton of money on decorations, as they always go above and beyond for their many themed nights. My favorite one so far has been "Under the Sea," which made it seem like you were partying in a coral reef. The Scorpio is another option, but I recommend going on a Friday night if you want to try it out. Fridays tend to have a better crowd than Saturday. There are drag shows at The Bar At 316 on Saturday nights and The Scorpio on Friday and Saturday nights. Chasers, a NoDa gay bar, has some weeknight drag shows but is mainly known for their dancers. Certain Sundays throughout the year there are drag brunches at certain restaurants, which are ticketed events. These are always a fun and entertaining experience! Sunday nights there is an LGBTQ themed night at Lost And Found, an "upscale neighborhood bar" just outside of Uptown. Lost And Found has neon signs, artificial grass walls, and a really fun DJ. The cocktails and unique and the atmosphere is perfect for pictures.

14. NODA IS PERFECT FOR THE ARTSY TYPES

NoDa, an area of Charlotte just north of the city, has a rich culture in the arts. It's quaint but thriving, with unique murals, shops, and art galleries. The new Wooden Robot Brewery location in NoDa has a rooftop patio and has easy access from the light rail stop. Visit the original Cabo Fish Taco location in NoDa, which has been featured on Food Network's hit show Diner, Drive-Ins, and Dives with Guy Fieri.

>TOURIST

NoDa also has this unique cat coffee shop… yes, you read that right. Mac Tabby Cat Cafe lets you order a coffee and then play in a room full of cats. Love cats? This should definitely be on your Charlotte itinerary. Allergic or not a big cat lover like myself? Avoid this cat haven.

15. POP BAR

One of the unique places you can visit in NoDa is the Pop Bar, which makes their own popsicles you can customize with different dippings and coatings. My favorite is the birthday cake pop, which I dip half in white chocolate with sprinkles… yum! Pop Bar is mildly pricey but as a one-of-a-kind novelty shop it's worth it. The purple wall outside the building is a common place for people to take pictures for social media, showing off their delicious pop creations.

16. TAKE A BREATHER OR SOME PICTURES IN THE BEAUTIFUL ROMARE BEARDEN PARK

Romare Bearden is a beautiful park in the Third Ward district in Uptown. Nestled perfectly in between tall buildings and the BB&T Ballpark, the park has ample grass area with a lighted waterfall fountain and interactive musical exhibit. This is a gorgeous place for a picnic or to enjoy the city views. There are ample tables and benches to sit at too with some shade. The park is always kept in pristine condition, and is host to numerous events throughout the year.

17. CHARLOTTE KNIGHTS ARE AN INEXPENSIVE, FUN EXPERIENCE

The Charlotte Knights routinely lead minor league baseball in attendance because of their gorgeous BB&T Ballpark and the views it has of Charlotte's skyline. This is a great place to catch a baseball game

>TOURIST

without emptying out your wallet. The Knights are the AAA team for the Chicago White Sox, and solid tickets can be purchased for under $20 each. The third base side is the best part of the ballpark to sit at, as it provides the best view of the city skyline in the outfield. Concession prices are slightly cheaper than the industry norm, and ballpark still looks brand new even though it opened in 2014.

18. ENJOY THE POST-GAME FIREWORKS AT FRIDAY AND SATURDAY KNIGHTS' GAMES

There are post-game fireworks synchronized to music after every Friday and Saturday Charlotte Knights game. You'll see fireworks launched strategically from the outfield while everything from Britney Spears to U2 plays throughout the stadium! These make Friday and Saturday night games more popular for the Knights, but the fireworks can also be seen from Romare Bearden Park if you do not want to purchase tickets. Nearby bars like Graham Street Pub and Patio also have a solid view of the fireworks. The music the fireworks are synchronized to can pretty much only be heard from inside the stadium, so if you are looking for the total experience you should purchase a Charlotte Knights game ticket.

19. THE KNIGHTS HAVE THURSDAY AND SUNDAY PROMOTIONS TOO

If you can't make it to a Friday or Saturday game, the Knights still have other fun promotions. The Thirsty Thursday promotion has $3 domestic draft beers and $5 local craft beers, and following every Sunday game kids can can run the bases with Homer The Dragon (their mascot). They have a promotional calendar where you can check which promotions are going on for certain games, and they have plenty of celebrity meet and greet experiences too! I once met Ham Porter from The Sandlot movies at a Charlotte Knights game… I even heard him say the infamous "You're killin' me, Smalls!" line! The official website for the Charlotte Knights is where you can easily buy tickets and check the promotional calendar. Save time and purchase them online versus waiting in the box office line at the ticket windows.

>TOURIST

20. IF YOU PLAN AHEAD THE CAROLINA PANTHERS GAMES ARE ALWAYS FUN

There are only eight home regular season Panthers games, but if you plan your trip in advance and purchase game tickets the Panthers games are always a blast! The games are always sold out, so you will need to buy tickets well in advance to avoid the pricey re-sale markups. Not a Panthers fan? See if they are playing your favorite team here and plan a trip around the game! Tailgating is done at numerous nearby parking lots, but all of Uptown is buzzing whenever there's a Panthers game! The best spot to watch the Panthers game if you don't have tickets would be Slate in South End. This is the most popular and lively spot on game days, but it does get pretty packed. Get there early and make sure you can establish a good spot before the game starts. They have a ton of televisions with all the games on, so no need to worry if you are a fan of another team. The sound will be on the Panthers game while they are playing, but there are "signature" team bars for most other NFL teams in Charlotte. I always watch the Philadelphia Eagles games at Big Ben's Pub in South

End, which is a popular meet up spot for Eagles fans. Fitzgerald's in Uptown is big Pittsburgh Steelers bar, and Tavern on the Tracks in South End is a year-round Buffalo sports bar. It's really cool to have any type of themed bar you can think of in Charlotte.

21. GRAHAM STREET PUB AND PATIO IS A REALLY COOL SPOT FOR A PREGAME DRINK

Graham Street Pub and Patio is located right between BB&T Ballpark (home of the Knights) and Bank Of America Stadium (home of the Panthers). This two-story bar and restaurant has a rooftop patio and plenty of beers on tap. This is a popular and lively spot to grab a drink before or after any Charlotte Knights or Carolina Panthers game. The rooftop patio has a great view of the city skyline and is a perfect spot to watch the sunset. They also have a food menu, but it is more known for casual drinks than for dinner. Try their new mixed drink that includes flavored vodka, soda, and a spiked seltzer all in one! It sounds more intense than it is, the taste is pretty awesome.

>TOURIST

22. LATTA ARCADE / THE FRENCH QUARTER IS UNIQUE AND FUN

Charlotte mainly has tall, modern glass buildings but located right between them is the Latta Arcade area many locals call "The French Quarter." This alleyway is directly across from Romare Bearden Park, and has classic old-fashioned buildings with white lights strung across the walkway. It's home to some unique spots to grab lunch and plenty of "hole in the wall" bars that have been there for decades. Definitely worth a visit, but some of the food spots are only open during lunch hours. Clover Joe's is my favorite lunch spot here, their sandwiches and hand-cut fries are to die for! Valhalla is a cafe at the corner of Latta Arcade that is open for dinner as well. This spot is quaint but popular, and they do take reservations for large parties, so call ahead to avoid the wait!

23. ZABLONG IS OPEN LATE AND DELICIOUS

Zablong Peculiar Pizza is located inside the Latta Arcade area and is a great spot to grab pizza. It's a long, oval-shaped personal pizza where you can customize it with as many toppings as you'd like. (Think Chipotle, but for pizza). It's open late, perfect for those late night cravings. The pizzas can be a bit pricey at over $11, but they are very filling and difficult to finish with just one person. You can add as many toppings as you'd like to your pizzas, and I've seen some people make some interesting combinations. I personally get the plain cheese pizza which has a discounted price of about $7, but I'm definitely in the minority. I highly recommend making your own pizza masterpiece while you're exploring Uptown Charlotte!

>TOURIST

24. CHARLOTTE HAS SOME AWESOME IRISH BARS

Like most cities, there are plenty of Irish bars in Charlotte owned and ran by 100% Irish employees. Latta Arcade is home to a few - Belfast Mill and Hooligan's being the most noteworthy- while Connoly's (Uptown) and Tyber Creek (South End) are other popular Irish spots. Belfast Mill and Hooligan's are more quaint and intimate while Connoly's and Tyber Creek are more lively. Belfast Mill is my favorite spot when I want to grab a casual drink, the bartenders are always super friendly. There is a big Notre Dame crowd for their games during the college football season. They normally have some pretty good drink specials too, make sure to check the specials board before ordering. There is never a cover at Belfast Mill or Hooligan's, but Connoly's does sometimes have a $5 entry fee. You simply can't visit Connoly's without taking an Irish Car Bomb shot, which sounds a lot worse than it is… it goes down super easily!

25. CHARLOTTE'S EPICENTRE IS A FUN SPOT

The EpiCentre, located in the heart of Uptown, is a diverse complex home to plenty of fun attractions. This is a hot spot for nightlife, restaurants, and the Studio Movie Grill movie theater. You'll find noteworthy names like Howl At The Moon, Tin Roof, and Whiskey River that are always busy. World Of Beer is a beer drinker's paradise with a ridiculous amount of beers on tap. Ask them about their rotating local options, and they always let you try the beers before ordering. Strike City is a bowling alley that is fun for a group outing. Studio Movie Grill is a movie theater that serves full-course meals to your seat. The Red Eye Diner is your 1950's style diner with reasonable prices and delicious food. It's open 24/7 too! I do not recommend going to Red Eye Diner late at night on the weekends, as you get the drunk crowd coming from the bars which can be annoying as you can imagine. It's a great spot any other time of the day and popular for lunch. There are more common lunch options, like Moe's Southwestern Grill and Five Guys Burgers and Fries. The Rocket Fizz candy store in the EpiCentre has all those classic candies you remember from your childhood but haven't seen since. They have unique sodas and drinks you can't find anywhere else. Best of all… you can mix and match candies while filling your own candy bags too! Definitely stop by this fun store while walking around the EpiCentre, it's even open late!

26. THE EPICENTRE IS NOT FAMILY FRIENDLY AFTER 9PM THURSDAY – SATURDAY

The nightlife starts to take off after 9pm on Thursday, Friday, and Saturday nights. After this time the complex is 21+ and it's definitely not a family-friendly environment. If you are enjoying a movie or bowling, make sure not to stay too late on these nights if you want to avoid the partying atmosphere. If you are looking for partying, this is one of the best spots in Charlotte for it. All the restaurants and even the Studio Movie Grill movie theater turn into bars with club atmospheres. There's lots of dancing and plenty of spots to grab drinks. Rooftop 210 is on the top floor, and for many reasons is by far my favorite bar inside the EpiCentre! Howl At The Moon is a piano bar, so if that is your thing it's usually pretty busy.

27. ROOFTOP 210 RARELY HAS A COVER

The big name chains like Tin Roof, Howl At The Moon, and Whiskey River usually have covers of $10+ on most weekends. Rooftop 210, a mainly outdoor bar with amazing views of the city, rarely has any cover. The music is typically modern with a DJ, and it's a fun place to dance the night away! I highly recommend going here on a Saturday night, it's usually more fun than those other more expensive bars that neighbor it in Charlotte's EpiCentre.

28. FUJI HAS THE BEST TAKEOUT HIBACHI

Want Hibachi but don't want to pay a high price? Fuji is located on the second floor of the EpiCentre and has amazing Hibachi takeout for under $10. You can watch the chef cooking the food on the grill behind the register once you order, so it's not some sketchy takeout situation. My personal favorite is the Hibachi chicken, I could eat it every single meal it's that good! This is the perfect lunch spot if you find yourself in Uptown and are in the mood for some Hibachi.

29. JOHNNY BURRITO IS A LEGENDARY CHARLOTTE LUNCH SPOT

Located in the underground portion of the Wells Fargo building, this local treasure is a Chipotle-style burrito place open only during lunch hours during the week. You'll probably wait in a long line (a clear sign of how popular this place is) but it moves quickly. Unlike Chipotle, you pay up front and can load up your burrito with as many toppings as you'd like without the extra fees for queso or quac. Johnny, the owner, gives out Atomic Fireballs for "Fireball Friday" and loves when you pay in cash. Tell him it is your first time and you'll get a "rookie card" while he rings the bell. It's essentially VIP treatment down the burrito assembly line and Johnny gives you a keychain as well. If you are really hungry I recommend the "grande por favor" which is the biggest burrito I've ever had! If you are a burrito lover, ditch Chipotle or Qdoba as this simply HAS to be on your itinerary for a weekday lunch spot!

30. OMNI HOTEL COIN BAR HAS A PUBLIC ROOFTOP POOL

Omni Hotel has a rooftop bar and pool, called Coin Bar, and is open to the public after 5pm. They offer unique cocktails at reasonable prices. This is the only rooftop pool open to the public in Charlotte. Coin Bar has a massive television screen, a clean pool, and even a few cornhole sets. It has a new, modern design to it that gives it a fresh vibe compared to typical bars. Rooftop pools like this one are a ton of fun and provide amazing city skyline views while you swim. You simply can't beat it! This is a fun stop for any summer visit!

>TOURIST

31. MERCHANT AND TRADE IS AN UPSCALE ROOFTOP BAR PERFECT FOR DRINKS

Merchant And Trade, located on the roof of the Tryon Park Hotel across from Romare Bearden Park, is an upscale cocktail bar with a great view. This is a perfect spot to watch the sunset while sipping some drinks with loved ones or friends. Make sure to dress somewhat nice, as most people will be wearing collared shirts. The lights, decor, and the atmosphere is top notch, with some slick lights to really put the aesthetic over the top. The signature cocktails are pricey, so make sure you keep that in mind when ordering. I usually only get one drink at Merchant and Trade while I enjoy the atmosphere and views, then head somewhere else for cheaper drinks. Belfast Mill and the other bars inside the Latta Arcade area are all right next door.

32. CITY LIGHTS IS ANOTHER GREAT ROOFTOP COCKTAIL BAR

City Lights, a rooftop cocktail bar on the top of Le Meridien Hotel, has a more panoramic view of the city skyline. Located on the edge of Uptown, the view is more comprehensive than that of Merchant and Trade, which is in the middle of the city. Charlotte buildings all have really cool light packages, making the nighttime view even more amazing. City Lights is one of the best "full picture" views you can get. The dress code is slightly dressy, but as long as you do not look sloppy you will be just fine. The prices are modest compared to other upscale cocktail bars. There is plenty of space and usually some good music playing, so if you are looking for city views while enjoying a nice cocktail, this should be your place!

33. TAKE IT BACK TO THE 90'S AT ROXBURY NIGHTCLUB

Charlotte has plenty of specialty themed bars. Roxbury, decorated and themed after the movie A

>TOURIST

Night At The Roxbury, is a complete 90's experience. You will seriously feel like you stepped back into the 90's, as you dance the night away to all the classics. There are televisions with the music videos playing to really give the full 90's affect. There's an arcade upstairs and dance floor downstairs, but it is usually easier to get a drink at the upstairs bar than downstairs. It can get a bit crowded down there. Roxbury typically has a $5 cover on Fridays and $7 cover on Saturdays, but if you are looking for a 1990's experience there aren't many places like it. Just be prepared to only hear the throwbacks, because they do not play any modern songs… it's all 90's all the time. Don't forget your glow sticks!

34. DANDELION MARKET IS ONE OF THE MOST POPULAR PLACES IN CHARLOTTE

Directly next to Roxbury, Dandelion Market is a restaurant during the daytime that turns into a nightclub after dark. The cover is normally $5 (cheaper than Roxbury's $7 on Saturdays) and the upstairs dance floor is a lot of fun with modern music.

If you need a drink, the bar downstairs is definitely easier to maneuver than the one upstairs. Saturday nights are the busiest for Dandelion Market, and it can get a decently long line for entry. The cover charge is always cash only, but they take cards inside for drinks. Make sure you check the specials board, because they usually have some pretty awesome drink specials. Last month they had $5 Kettle One vodka!

35. CHARLOTTE HORNETS GAMES ARE FUN AND NOT CRAZY EXPENSIVE

The Charlotte Hornets are not a historically great team, so it makes the games somewhat more affordable than NBA teams in other cities. The games are still a fun experience, especially if they are playing a premiere opponent. With 41 home games, these are more accessible and affordable than Panthers games. The Spectrum Center they play in is directly across from the EpiCentre, so it makes it easy for pre or post game drinks and food. I typically stop at World Of Beer for a drink or two before heading across the street into the game.

>TOURIST

36. ATTENDING A HORNETS GAME? FITZGERALD'S IS ALSO A GREAT PREGAME SPOT FOR FOOD AND DRINKS

Fitzgerald's, an Irish sports restaurant and bar, is located next to the Spectrum Center (home of the Hornets). It's a great place to grab some food and drinks before you head over to the game, as prices inside the arena are definitely inflated. The chicken fingers are amazing at Fitzgerald's! There's plenty of seating but it does get busy on Hornets game days. There are plenty of drink specials, so make sure your check them out or ask about them before ordering. The outdoor patio is really nice when the weather permits, but these tables tend to go fast when the temperatures are in the 70's - 80's.

37. UNC CHARLOTTE HAS A SCENIC CAMPUS YOU SHOULD VISIT

Located in the University section of Charlotte, just north of the city, UNC Charlotte is a beautiful campus that is perfect for a relaxing afternoon stroll. The lavish brick buildings with tall white columns provide a picturesque campus along with the red brick walking paths. You'll see the Southern charm of the buildings similar to other college campuses in the Southeast region. I highly recommend getting some steps in while you enjoy the beauty this campus has to offer. There is a nature trail open to the public that is worth checking out. There are rarely many people on campus on the weekends, so take your time and enjoy the natural beauty. The red brick pathway that goes alongside the track and field complex and soccer fields is really scenic with landscaping that is always top notch.

>TOURIST

38. UNC CHARLOTTE FOOTBALL GAMES ARE FUN AND CHEAP

UNC Charlotte may not have a noteworthy football program, but they still have a fun game day atmosphere that is extremely affordable. Ticket prices are typically under $15, and it's a fun way to enjoy college football with your whole family. The stadium is not massive, so there really isn't a bad seat in the house. I recommend picking a game later in the season if possible, because it can get ridiculously hot at some of the early season games. When the temperature is in the 90's it's no fun with the metal bleachers in direct sunlight. If you are with any young children, avoid the student tailgate lot near the North Deck. Things can get a bit rowdy in the student tailgate zone, but it is not somewhere you'd pass through on your way to the stadium, it's off by itself. If you are looking to tailgate, there are options in the parking deck that you can rent out for a game. The top floors of the parking deck are usually the first to fill up, so make sure you arrive early if you are looking to tailgate.

UNC Charlotte isn't the most impressive tailgate, but the overall experience and the price is perfect for families not trying to break the bank.

39. WORKMAN'S FRIEND HAS PHENOMENAL GRILLED CHEESE AND TOMATO SOUP

Workman's Friend, an Irish restaurant and bar in Plaza Midwood, is a lively spot at all times of the day. Locals frequent this spot for lunch and dinner, as well as after hours for drinks and Irish coffees. Their grilled cheese and tomato soup is one of the most popular dishes on the menu, and it's a MUST for any grilled cheese lover. The vibe changes around 9pm from casual restaurant to lively bar with a bouncer. The drinks are moderately priced and there is usually a live music performance or DJ to keep the mood energetic.

>TOURIST

40. ROSEMONT HAS ADULT CAPRISUN STYLE DRINKS

Rosemont, a South End bar and restaurant, has amazing alcoholic drinks served in Caprisun style pouches. My personal favorite is the Transfusion - a blend of grape juice, vodka, and Sprite. Rosemont also has spiked milkshakes and phenomenal buffalo chicken macaroni and cheese. The spiked milkshakes are very filling but delicious, so if you are traveling maybe you can make an exception from your typical diet to try one. The atmosphere is lit with neon lights, and there is usually a band performing inside. Highly recommend stopping at Rosemont for a meal or some drinks! The band can make it a bit noisy inside, so if you are looking for a quiet meal this might not be your best option. Usually a band is performing on Thursday, Friday, and Saturday nights. There are drink specials, and Fridays are really popular with their $3 wells (house liquor) special. This place has some of the most unique drinks in Charlotte, so it's worth checking out while you are here!

41. SOUTH PARK MALL IS A PREMIERE SHOPPING DESTINATION

The South Park Mall in the South Park region of Charlotte is honestly one of the nicer malls I've ever visited. It's loaded with designer stores like Louis Vuitton and Tiffany's while still having the usual mall favorites like Bath and Body Works. New stores are constantly opening up to keep the variation fresh, and it even has a Cheesecake Factory location. Untuckit and Casper are just two examples of new stores that have opened up at the South Park Mall within the past few months. The mall is in a wealthier part of Charlotte, with beautiful homes and plenty of restaurants nearby. I love that the South Park Mall has a Vineyard Vines location, which you can get a souvenir Vineyard Vines Charlotte t-shirt at if you also love the brand. Any shopping fan will find this area of Charlotte to be as close to paradise as they can find in the state of North Carolina. It seriously has almost any store you can think of!

>TOURIST

42. QUAIL HOLLOW SHOULD BE ON THE BUCKET LIST FOR ANY GOLFER

Are you a golfer? Quail Hollow is home to the Wells Fargo Championship every year, which draws some big names on the PGA Tour. It also was home to the 2017 PGA Championship, and is hands down the best golf course in the Charlotte area. Even if you are not able to play the course, the neighborhood surrounding it is full of beautiful architecture and views. I remember watching Justin Thomas win his first ever major here in 2017 at the PGA Championship. The Wells Fargo Championship each May is always a popular attraction at this gorgeous golf course and country club.

43. BALLANTYNE CORPORATE PARK HAS PLENTY OF SCENIC WALKING TRAILS

Located in South Charlotte, Ballantyne Corporate Park is home to over 300 companies, including the headquarters for Fortune 500 companies. The 2,000 acre property has gorgeous landscaping and plenty of walking trails. Couples often have engagement pictures done on the grounds, and it's a popular spot for runners and walkers alike. I highly recommend going on a walk or run through these scenic grounds. You'll definitely recognize some of the company names with offices in the corporate park, from TIAA to Snyder-Lance to ESPN's SEC Network. It's a beautiful and relaxing place for an afternoon stroll. Make sure you take the path that leads down by the ponds and fountains… it's natural beauty and serenity makes it my favorite walking path in the Ballantyne area.

>TOURIST

44. ALEXANDER MICHAEL'S "WHAT IT IS" DISH MUST BE TRIED

Alexander Michael's is a quaint restaurant located just outside Uptown. The building is an old Victorian home that is in a neighborhood with some beautiful houses. "Al Mike's" (as locals call it) is always busy and does not take reservations, so make sure you go earlier than normal to avoid a massive crowd. They do require that your entire party is present at the time of seating to make sure they turn tables as quickly as possible. They are very strict about this policy, so definitely make sure everyone in your party is present when they call your name. Their most popular dish is called the "What It Is," a blackened grilled chicken breast over rotini in a cajun cream sauce. It's one of the best dishes in all of Charlotte! Al Mike's is very pretty around Christmas time, and it almost looks like a neighborhood that could be in a Hallmark Christmas movie.

45. BENNY PENNELLO'S PIZZA IS MASSIVE... LITERALLY

Benny Pennello's is home to the 28 inch pizza, and sells it by the slice. These slices are absolutely massive and take multiple plates to hold. My favorite is the traditional pepperoni, but they have all types of pizza for the more adventurous taste buds. Benny Pennello's is open late too, perfect for any late night cravings. If you are looking to feed a large group, they do have massive pizzas you can order to go. My only complaint with the 28 inch pizza is that the box is so massive it is difficult to fit it through doors and in your car. It's seriously that big!

46. SOUTH END'S CHARLOTTE RAIL TRAIL IS A HOTSPOT

The Charlotte Rail Trail runs alongside the light rail tracks, and is a paved pathway for pedestrians and plenty of electric scooters. There are numerous restaurants and breweries along the trail, so it's a perfect way to get exercise in while you make some fun pit stops. There is street art painted along the trail,

>TOURIST

including a colorful "carpet" painting on the pavement. I typically walk down the trail with friends and stop at Sycamore Brewing, Suffolk Punch, and Triple C Brewing. These are all just off the trail and fun to visit. I also make sure to grab an ice cream at Jenis, which is just across the street from the pathway. The trail goes on for miles, so there's plenty of opportunity to work off those calories! I also enjoy running along this trail in the mornings, especially if you can enjoy the sunrise during your run.

47. THE U.S. NATIONAL WHITEWATER CENTER IS A FUN DESTINATION FOR THE DAY

The U.S. National Whitewater Center has plenty of fun adventures for you to go on. Whether you are whitewater rafting, ziplining, or rock wall climbing, this massive complex has it all. There are food and drink options, but it's also fun to bring your picnic supplies and eat along the water currents. The stage is host to bands in the evening, and this place is always lively on any Saturday or Sunday. Make sure you bring sunscreen if it's during the summer months, as the majority of this complex is in the sun. If you are looking for thrills, this is the place to be. Purchase the unlimited all-day pass and enjoy as much ziplining, rock wall climbing, and whitewater rafting as you can handle! This is truly a one-of-a-kind attraction and one of the most unique places to visit in Charlotte. Planning a visit around St. Patrick's Day? The U.S. National Whitewater Center turns the water green for their annual St. Patrick's Day celebration, it's an awesome sight to see!

48. TACO TUESDAY AT HOT TACO

Hot Taco is a trendy Mexican restaurant located on the Rail Trail, and it thrives on Taco Tuesday. Their taco specials attract big crowds, but you can put your name on the waitlist ahead of time on their website. Most people are not aware of this, so they end up waiting in person much longer than you would have to if you added your name to the list online. I highly recommend the queso dip, it's some of the best queso I've ever had! Parking can fill up in the lot across the street, so take the light rail, a ride share, or scooter if

>TOURIST

possible. Hot Taco is right on a light rail stop, so most people take advantage of this cheap mode of transportation.

49. THE CHARLOTTE CHECKERS GAMES ARE AFFORDABLE AND EXCITING

The Charlotte Checkers, the AHL team for the Carolina Hurricanes, play their games at the Bojangles Coliseum just outside of Uptown. These games are almost never sold out, as Charlotte is not a big hockey market. The team recently won the Calder Cup, and the games are always super fun and exciting - especially if you have never experienced a hockey game in person. Tickets are under $20 for decent seats, so it's an affordable activity that's fun for the whole family. Keep in mind that parking is normally between $5 and $10. Every seat is pretty close to the action, so there honestly isn't a bad seat in the Bojangles Coliseum. These games are always full of action, I highly recommend attending one while you are here!

50. THE BILLY GRAHAM LIBRARY IS A POPULAR TOURIST DESTINATION

The Billy Graham Library is a museum dedicated to the influential Billy Graham, a leader in faith. You can learn about his life and achievements and tour his family home. There is also food and a gift shop, it's a MUST for any history buffs or religious visitors. This is actually Yelp's highest-rated attraction for Charlotte, so give it a visit while you are here. Weekends are typically more crowded, so if you can, I'd recommend going on a weekday instead.

51. CHARLOTTE'S NEW OPTIMIST HALL IS A FOODIE'S DREAM

Optimist Hall, a reclaimed factory building, just opened in Charlotte. It's home to numerous food stalls, shops, and bars. The Dumpling Lady (dumplings) and Papi Queso (grilled cheese) opened their first stationary locations after the booming success of their food trucks. These locations have

\>TOURIST

been extremely popular among guests… and for good reason! You have to try the Mac Melt at Papi Queso, which combines macaroni and cheese into a grilled cheese sandwich. It's simply phenomenal! El Thrifty Social is a game lounge and bar that just opened up inside Optimist Hall. You can enjoy cocktails and drinks while candlepin bowling or playing shuffleboard. They have a delicious food menu and the prices are pretty reasonable. There is no additional fee to bowl or play any of the games, so grab some drinks with your group and have fun! I love challenging my friends to some friendly competition with candlepin bowling here, where the loser buys the next round of drinks! The atmosphere is perfect for clever Instagram pictures, if you're like me and always looking for that next photo opportunity.

>TOURIST

TOP REASONS TO BOOK THIS TRIP

Breweries: Charlotte's close to 50 local breweries are fun places to drink great beer, socialize with friends (and dogs), and play games.

Rooftop Bars: Charlotte has numerous rooftop bars that provide incredible views of the city skyline.

Food: Charlotte is home to many unique places to eat, with some incredible dishes you MUST try!

>TOURIST
OTHER RESOURCES:

Charlotte's Got A Lot Travel Website

Charlotte Regional Business Alliance Region Maps

Charlotte Culture Guide

Tripadvisor Charlotte Attractions

A Beer-Drinker's Map Of The 47 Charlotte-Area Breweries And What To Order There

10 Best Rooftop Bars In Charlotte

Carowinds Website, Where You Should Purchase Tickets Ahead of Time

U.S. National Whitewater Center

Charlotte LYNX Blue Line Routes And Schedules For Light Rail

University of North Carolina Charlotte Website And Information

Optimist Hall Information And Food Options

Charlotte's EpiCentre Attractions And Information

>TOURIST

PACKING AND PLANNING TIPS

A Week before Leaving

- Arrange for someone to take care of pets and water plants.
- Email and Print important Documents.
- Get Visa and vaccines if needed.
- Check for travel warnings.
- Stop mail and newspaper.
- Notify Credit Card companies where you are going.
- Passports and photo identification is up to date.
- Pay bills.
- Copy important items and download travel Apps.
- Start collecting small bills for tips.
- Have post office hold mail while you are away.
- Check weather for the week.
- Car inspected, oil is changed, and tires have the correct pressure.
- Check airline luggage restrictions.
- Download Apps needed for your trip.

Right Before Leaving

- Contact bank and credit cards to tell them your location.
- Clean out refrigerator.
- Empty garbage cans.
- Lock windows.
- Make sure you have the proper identification with you.
- Bring cash for tips.
- Remember travel documents.
- Lock door behind you.
- Remember wallet.
- Unplug items in house and pack chargers.
- Change your thermostat settings.
- Charge electronics, and prepare camera memory cards.

\>TOURIST

READ OTHER GREATER THAN A TOURIST BOOKS

Greater Than a Tourist- Geneva Switzerland: 50 Travel Tips from a Local by Amalia Kartika

Greater Than a Tourist- St. Croix US Birgin Islands USA: 50 Travel Tips from a Local by Tracy Birdsall

Greater Than a Tourist- San Juan Puerto Rico: 50 Travel Tips from a Local by Melissa Tait

Greater Than a Tourist – Lake George Area New York USA: 50 Travel Tips from a Local by Janine Hirschklau

Greater Than a Tourist – Monterey California United States: 50 Travel Tips from a Local by Katie Begley

Greater Than a Tourist – Chanai Crete Greece: 50 Travel Tips from a Local by Dimitra Papagrigoraki

Greater Than a Tourist – The Garden Route Western Cape Province South Africa: 50 Travel Tips from a Local by Li-Anne McGregor van Aardt

Greater Than a Tourist – Sevilla Andalusia Spain: 50 Travel Tips from a Local by Gabi Gazon

Children's Book: *Charlie the Cavalier Travels the World* by Lisa Rusczyk Ed. D.

> TOURIST

Follow us on Instagram for beautiful travel images:
http://Instagram.com/GreaterThanATourist

Follow *Greater Than a Tourist* on Amazon.
>Tourist Podcast
>T Website
>T Youtube
>T Facebook
>T Goodreads
>T Amazon
>T Mailing List
>T Pinterest
>T Instagram
>T Twitter
>T SoundCloud
>T LinkedIn
>T Map

> TOURIST

At *Greater Than a Tourist*, we love to share travel tips with you. How did we do? What guidance do you have for how we can give you better advice for your next trip? Please send your feedback to GreaterThanaTourist@gmail.com as we continue to improve the series. We appreciate your constructive feedback. Thank you.

>TOURIST

METRIC CONVERSIONS

TEMPERATURE

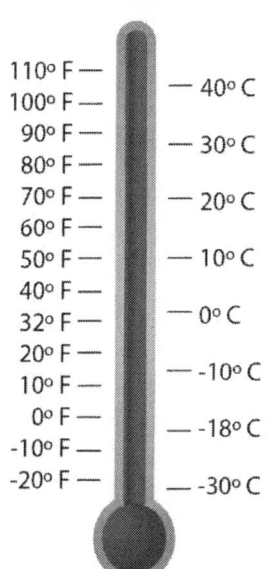

110° F — 40° C
100° F
90° F — 30° C
80° F
70° F — 20° C
60° F
50° F — 10° C
40° F
32° F — 0° C
20° F
10° F — -10° C
0° F
-10° F — -18° C
-20° F — -30° C

To convert F to C:
Subtract 32, and then multiply by 5/9 or .5555.

To Convert C to F:
Multiply by 1.8 and then add 32.

32F = 0C

LIQUID VOLUME

To Convert:..................Multiply by
U.S. Gallons to Liters................. 3.8
U.S. Liters to Gallons 26
Imperial Gallons to U.S. Gallons 1.2
Imperial Gallons to Liters....... 4.55
Liters to Imperial Gallons 22

1 Liter = .26 U.S. Gallon
1 U.S. Gallon = 3.8 Liters

DISTANCE

To convert ....Multiply by
Inches to Centimeters 2.54
Centimeters to Inches 39
Feet to Meters...................... .3
Meters to Feet 3.28
Yards to Meters 91
Meters to Yards 1.09
Miles to Kilometers 1.61
Kilometers to Miles............ .62

1 Mile = 1.6 km
1 km = .62 Miles

WEIGHT

1 Ounce = .28 Grams
1 Pound = .4555 Kilograms
1 Gram = .04 Ounce
1 Kilogram = 2.2 Pounds

\>TOURIST

TRAVEL QUESTIONS

- Do you bring presents home to family or friends after a vacation?

- Do you get motion sick?

- Do you have a favorite billboard?

- Do you know what to do if there is a flat tire?

- Do you like a sun roof open?

- Do you like to eat in the car?

- Do you like to wear sun glasses in the car?

- Do you like toppings on your ice cream?

- Do you use public bathrooms?

- Did you bring a cell phone and does it have power?

- Do you have a form of identification with you?

- Have you ever been pulled over by a cop?

- Have you ever given money to a stranger on a road trip?

- Have you ever taken a road trip with animals?

- Have you ever gone on a vacation alone?

- Have you ever run out of gas?

- If you could move to any place in the world, where would it be?
- If you could travel anywhere in the world, where would you travel?
- If you could travel in any vehicle, which one would it be?
- If you had three things to wish for from a magic genie, what would they be?
- If you have a driver's license, how many times did it take you to pass the test?
- What are you the most afraid of on vacation?
- What do you want to get away from the most when you are on vacation?
- What foods smell bad to you?
- What item do you bring on ever trip with you away from home?
- What makes you sleepy?
- What song would you love to hear on the radio when you're cruising on the highway?
- What travel job would you want the least?
- What will you miss most while you are away from home?
- What is something you always wanted to try?

>TOURIST

- What is the best road side attraction that you ever saw?
- What is the farthest distance you ever biked?
- What is the farthest distance you ever walked?
- What is the weirdest thing you needed to buy while on vacation?
- What is your favorite candy?
- What is your favorite color car?
- What is your favorite family vacation?
- What is your favorite food?
- What is your favorite gas station drink or food?
- What is your favorite license plate design?
- What is your favorite restaurant?
- What is your favorite smell?
- What is your favorite song?
- What is your favorite sound that nature makes?
- What is your favorite thing to bring home from a vacation?
- What is your favorite vacation with friends?
- What is your favorite way to relax?

- Where is the farthest place you ever traveled in a car?
- Where is the farthest place you ever went North, South, East and West?
- Where is your favorite place in the world?
- Who is your favorite singer?
- Who taught you how to drive?
- Who will you miss the most while you are away?
- Who if the first person you will contact when you get to your destination?
- Who brought you on your first vacation?
- Who likes to travel the most in your life?
- Would you rather be hot or cold?
- Would you rather drive above, below, or at the speed limited?
- Would you rather drive on a highway or a back road?
- Would you rather go on a train or a boat?
- Would you rather go to the beach or the woods?

>TOURIST

TRAVEL BUCKET LIST

1.

2.

3.

4.

5.

6.

7.

8.

9.

10.

>TOURIST
NOTES

Made in the USA
Columbia, SC
01 June 2022